DISCOVERING OLD OREGON SERIES

Volume Two

Oregon Coast

Joyce Herbst

FRANK AMATO PUBLICATIONS

Box 02112, Portland, Oregon 97202

(503) 653-8108

Dedicated to future generations who will enjoy the beauty of this wonderful Oregon coastline.

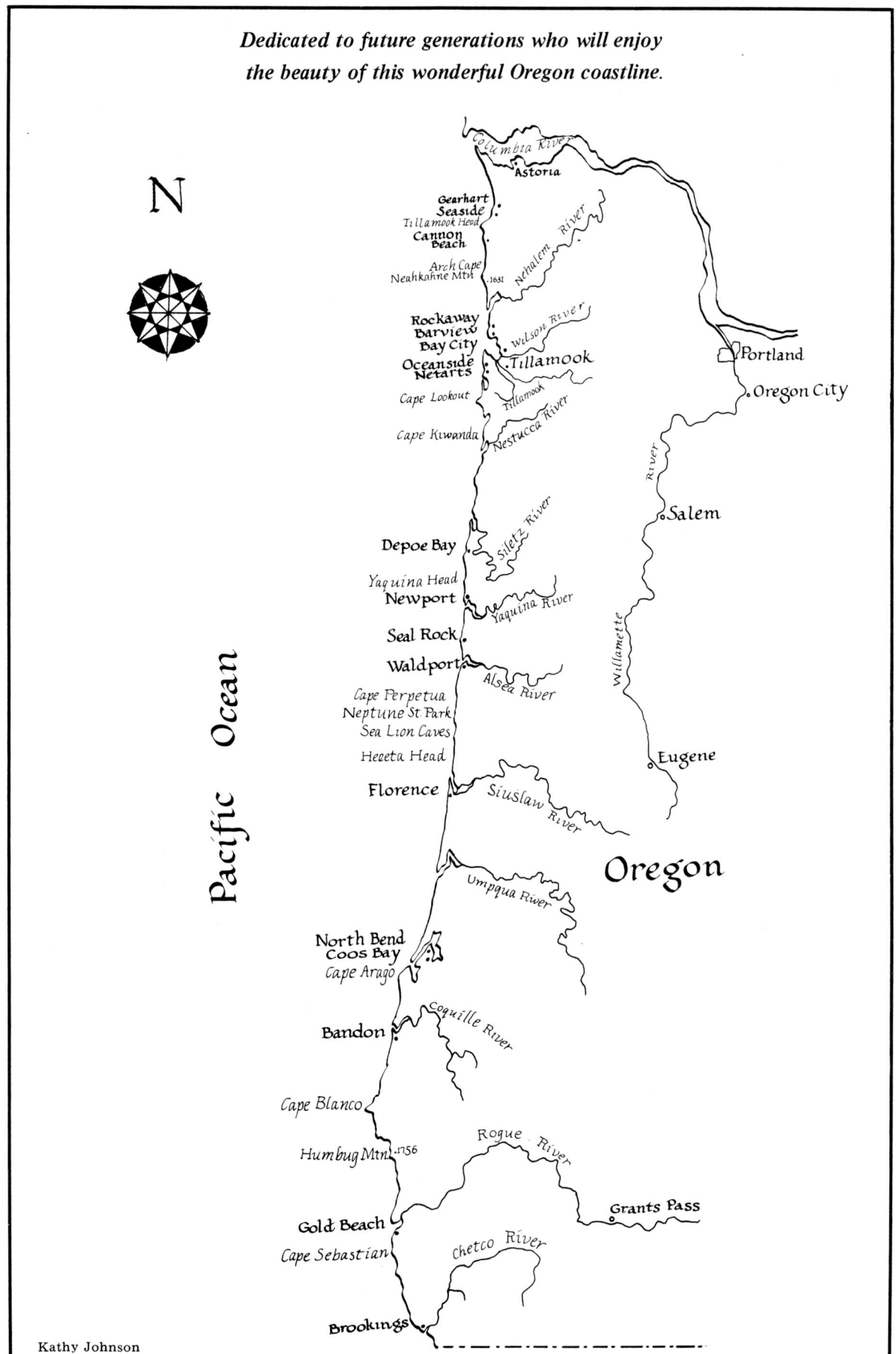

Kathy Johnson

Printed in U.S.A. Copyright 1985, Frank Amato Publications
ISBN 0-936608-32-3 softbound, 0-936608-331 hardbound.
Typesetting: Chris Mazzuca

Oregon Coast

Shoshone warriors called the evergreen land where the River of the West flowed *Oyer-un-gun*. The Canadian traders called it *Wa-ure-gan*, meaning "beautiful water." The Spanish adventurers called it *Aqua-Aura*, meaning "gently flowing water," and from these came the name Oregon.

There are almost four-hundred miles of shoreline along the Oregon Coast featuring some of the most spectacular scenery in the world. The most northern city is Astoria, the oldest American city west of the Mississippi River. There you find the mouth of the Columbia River which serves as a shipping highway to Oregon, Washington and Idaho ports, the four-and-one-half-mile long Astoria Bridge, Astor Column and many old Victorian homes. Nearly one-half the population of this fishing town is of Finnish descent.

Each town along the coast has its own unique qualities. Highway 101 takes you from Astoria to the southernmost city of Brookings, following the coastline most of the way. The main industries of the region are fishing, timber and tourism. The coast has many excellent fishing areas and hiking trails from which you can see the battered shoreline and white beaches with numerous inlets for beachcombing and exploring tide pools.

Flora such as rhododendron, azalea and salal are abundant all along the coast. There are a variety of rivers, low mountains and valleys with numerous wildlife and bird species. You can often see herds of sea lions and seals. Pods of spouting whales can be seen in December and January. The large variety of trees growing along the coast includes Douglas fir, hemlock, Sitka spruce, Port Orford cedar and one tree that is found only in southwest Oregon, the myrtle. Its wood is used to make jewelry and household articles and is sold in most gift shops along the coast.

The protective loyalty of Oregonians for their coast is shown in the legislation which has been passed to correct such abuses as driving on beaches, litter and keeping the beaches open for public use.

Oregon's state park system is one of the most extensive in the western states. There are nearly ten thousand camp and picnic sites and several hundred state parks with a great many of these along the coast.

Before the white man came the Oregon Coast was home to a score of Indian tribes. Today the coast reflects very little of their rich history. However the beauty of the coast remains and its feeling for many of us is summed up in this poem by John Masefield:

I must go down to the sea again
to the lonely sea and the sky,
And all I ask is a tall ship
And a star to steer her by.

Joyce Herbst

Astoria was named after John Jacob Astor, a New York businessman, who had it established as a fur trading center in 1811. It was so named until 1813 when the British renamed it Fort George. Fort George remained until 1818 when it was returned to the United States and renamed Astoria. The 150' by 200' Fort was of substantial size for that day. The drawing below was published in the Illustrated London News, *February 10, 1849, and shows what the area looked like around 1813.*

FORT GEORGE OR ASTORIA, COLUMBIA RIVER.—THE HUDSON'S BAY COMPANY'S ESTABLISHMENT.

Saloons, such as this one in Astoria, were often meeting places for loggers, merchants, farmers, sailors and fishermen. In the evenings drinking was often boisterous as rough men on a spending spree looked for heavy drinking and exciting entertainment.

The Weinhard Beer Company delivery truck in Astoria. Later it would merge to become the Blitz Weinhard Company.

Each year millions of salmon and steelhead returned to the Columbia River including genetic races of chinook salmon which sometimes weighed over 80 pounds. The large chinook pictured was such a special fish; its progeny are almost extinct in the Columbia River because of dams, irrigation withdrawals and pollution. The importance of salmon to early explorers, fur trappers and settlers is underscored by the fact that the largest species of salmon was named after the original Indian inhabitants of the lower Columbia — the Chinooks.

A square-rigger anchored off Tongue Point on the Columbia River near Astoria. Tongue Point was the first geographic feature to be named by explorers which did not directly face the Pacific Coast.

In July of 1924 a devastating fire destroyed many blocks of downtown Astoria. Wood constructed buildings burned rapidly and quickly got out of control, overtaxing small firefighting units lacking adequate equipment. Severe fires of this sort were common occurrences in the early wood constructed towns along the coast.

Thousands of gillnet/sailboats were used in the late 1880s near Astoria. Pictured are Ludwig Larsen and stepson Edward Erickson.

Salmon in the round await cleaning and sorting. Harvest, with little thought about conservation, was the name of the game as the coastal fishing industry grew. In 1909 the sport limit on crabs was 50 sacks per day per person!

Because they would work for low wages, Chinese employees filled the fish canneries. The hardest job was cleaning the fish – removing the head, fins and entrails. Around the turn of the century, an anti-Chinese prejudiced white invented what quickly became known as the "Iron Chink." It was a contraption that beheaded and cleaned salmon in one quick mechanical motion. It displaced Chinese labor (as its prejudiced inventor wanted it to do).

Pioneers had ways of exploiting Oregon's resources such as seining. Horse teams hauled in huge nets of salmon along the Columbia and Rogue rivers; each year fewer fish returned to the rivers.

From 1865 until 1900 the commercial salmon gillnet fleet grew from a couple of boats to over 2500. The "Butterfly Fleet," as it has been called, was manned by rugged individuals from all along the Pacific Coast. As the runs progressed from river to river many traveling fishermen would follow them. Near the turn of the century, Astoria had a reputation for being a hard drinking, hard carousing town.

Two men were required to work each boat, one on the oars and the other with the net. By 1915 the Butterfly Fleet had become completely extinct with sails giving way to gasoline, motor-powered boats capable of being operated by one man.

Women played a valuable part in the cannery work force. Indian women helped clean the fish and others put on labels, as the ladies shown here are doing. Both were tedious jobs and usually called for long hours in rather uncomfortable positions.

Spring chinook were the most valuable fish caught in the lower Columbia near Astoria. They were very large and had the finest flavor because of their mint condition. As the spring chinook runs declined in size, the commercial fishery zeroed in on runs of smaller size sockeye, chum and coho salmon as well as steelhead trout. Even before the turn of the century Columbia River chinook were being sold to customers around the world. This fish cannery photograph was taken about 1915.

The Peter Iredale, a 278-foot British four mast bark wrecked on Clatsop Beach October 25, 1906. The Point Adams lifesaving crew helped all hands safely to shore. During World War II the only enemy shell to strike Oregon soil landed near the Peter Iredale. The ship has remained partly buried in the sand for over a half-century and has become a major tourist attraction and the most photographed shipwreck on the Pacific Coast.

BRITISH BARQUE PETER IREDALE, WRECKED 1906

The beach was the best highway available and was used as such. Sometimes the "tin lizzy" was not the best means of travel, though, and many times a horse and buggy would be required to pull a car out of the sand, much to the embarrassment of its owner!

The Hotel Gearhart, just north of Seaside, was a favorite vacation spot for Portlanders until its demise.

Razor clams are tasty and always a challenge to find. Northern Oregon beaches were once filled with these clams but overharvest, pollution, and auto travel on the beach have destroyed many of the beds.

The "cigar raft" was made by strapping logs together in a cylinder shape. These rafts were towed from the Northwest to San Francisco or other California mill towns. The rafts moved very slowly but could transport a million board feet or more at once.

Some coastal scenes remain the same such as this beautiful evening photo at Twin Rocks.

This photo of the main street in Seaside taken in about 1890 shows a typical street scene of that period with dirt roads, livery stable, wooden walks, and horsedrawn buggies. Seaside developed into one of Oregon's largest resort towns by the 1920s.

Pacific Northwest forests were filled with both mystery and adventure. Explorers often referred to the "nearly inexhaustible supply of timber" where massive fir, hemlock, spruce and cedar trees crowded the shore as shown in this 1892 photo taken at the Myricle Estate near Seaside.

The coastal Indian tribes numbered approximately 45,000 before the white man came. Around the beginning of the nineteenth century the Indian population decreased rapidly, mainly from introduced diseases. The Chinook tribe was reduced to one-tenth of its original size. The Chinook jargon was used by the coast tribes and those along the Columbia River as a highly useful language. The fish hook, spear, scoopnet and canoe were essential for the coastal tribes and were designed and perfected over thousands of years into very efficient tools. Many white men failed in their attempts to supply their ships with fish using hooks and methods other than those of the Indians and eventually turned to them to supply the ship while in that area. The picture here is of oyster pickers on their way home.

This picture, taken in 1921, shows Seaside as a busy resort town with its gift shops, swimming beaches and beautiful 8000-foot promenade that is still used today.

The name Seaside came from the famous hotel resort, the Seaside House, pictured here. The turnaround is officially designated as the end of the Lewis and Clark Trail.

Seaside's patriotism ran high during World War II. This signboard shows where some of our men were fighting.

Bathers near Gearhart in 1910 showing off some of the swim wear popular in that day. Though dressed in rather cumbersome attire, all seem to be having a good time.

Haystack Rock is the third largest monolith in the world and one of the most photographed areas along the coast. The area surrounding it is restricted to protect the sea life in its natural habitat.

It is always irresistible to wade in the surf, though the water is very cold, even in mid-summer.

The schooner Shark wrecked while leaving the Columbia River on September 10, 1846, and part of her deck with a small cannon drifted ashore providing the name Cannon Beach. (The cannon is still there.) Haystack Rock is a 235 foot tourist attraction with an eight-mile stretch of beach used for swimming, necessitating the lifeguards as shown in this 1951 photo.

Sand carving has always been an enjoyable pastime and some creations are more elaborate than others. These historic faces were carved at Seaside in the 1920s. There is still an annual competition at Cannon Beach which draws large numbers of contestants and spectators.

After many futile landing attempts, the construction of the Tillamook Lighthouse was started in October, 1879, and completed in January of 1881, costing $123,493 to build. Over 29 feet of rock was blasted away to make a platform for the station. The rock was a mile from shore and 80 feet high with a sharp overhang, making it necessary to land supplies with a derrick. In September of 1957 the light was replaced by a radar buoy and the rock and lighthouse were designated as surplus property and eventually sold to two men from Las Vegas in 1959. It was sold again in 1980 for use as a columbarium — a repository for ashes of cremated persons.

Barview, named in 1884 by L. C. Smith, is located just north of the bar at the entrance to Tillamook Bay and is subject to extremely fierce weather conditions, including this storm in 1915 which destroyed many houses and the railroad bed and tracks.

This scene at Rockaway shows it as a compact little town with the train station only a few feet from the wooden main street with its shops and restaurant. It even had a vegetable garden next to the railroad. All in all, a very pleasant place to be.

Around 1850 Henry W. Wilson was the first man to bring cattle to the Tillamook area, laying the foundation for its great dairy industry. The Wilson River was named in his honor. In 1890 Tillamook County produced about one-hundred tons of butter, one-third of which was consumed in the county. In 1891, Merriman Foland started the first commercial cheese making venture. Named father of the cheddar cheese industry was a Scotsman, Peter McIntosh, who arrived in Tillamook in 1894. Many honors were awarded to the dairymen, such as depicted in this photo.

There have always been pretty girls to photograph on the beach as shown in this photo taken sometime in the 1930s at Rockaway.

In the old days fish limits were very liberal, leading to overharvest and depleted runs. These three fishermen on the Antelope *have a catch comprised of adult chinook salmon (lying near the stern of the boat), sea-run cutthroat trout and tiny, pre-migrant steelhead trout. In the fall after the first rains, runs of coho and chinook salmon as well as sea-run cutthroat trout, ascend all of Oregon's coastal rivers as they have done for tens of thousands of years. In December, runs of winter steelhead arrive and continue into the spring. This rich variety of fish runs makes the Oregon Coast one of the world's premier sport fisheries. In 1924 there was a $75.00 fine for wasting salmon; other limits in the years following helped protect the fisheries.*

Early roads were sometimes covered with wooden planks to make the going easier in wet weather. During the long rainy season, coach travel was horrible on muddy, rut-filled roads. In this photo a huge old growth tree has almost blocked the road.

Wagons and coaches were a necessity and came in a variety of styles. Springless "mud wagons" were used on mountainous roads because they were less apt to turn over. The "jerky" was a two-seated wagon. The Concord Coach was sturdily built so the passenger section rolled rather than jerked on rough ground. By 1914 roads had improved enough that auto travel was supplanting the stagecoach. This was also the last year the stage ran from Yamhill to Tillamook, as shown in this photo.

Snow along the coast is unusual but sometimes does occur. This photo taken at Tillamook in the 1920s shows one of the few snow storms which almost closed down the town.

Gillnetting salmon and steelhead was done in coastal rivers until the Oregon State legislature banned it, thus helping to preserve the runs of fish.

In 1913 heavy snows in the Coast Range prevented coach travel from Yamhill for over three months. Mail piled up and was finally sent by the Portland Steamer, Sue Elmore, *to Tillamook, where it was stacked on the street.*

Early loggers used oxen to pull downed trees to mills or streams on skid roads. Skids were laid like railroad ties, a few feet apart, and greased. When the oxen dragged the logs across them they would smoke and sometimes catch fire from the friction.

The easiest way to move logs was in the water. It was a dangerous job, calling for good judgment and quick reflexes. Here a whole family and their pet pose for a picture.

This type of crib trestle was not only a sturdy structure but a practical one as well because it could be taken apart and hauled out as logs when the camp was moved.

Two-hundred and ninety-thousand acres containing half a billion feet of merchantable fir, cedar and hemlock were burned in August of 1933. The fire spread to within eight miles of the town of Tillamook before being stopped by rain and thousands of men fighting it for over four days.

The sad aftermath of the Tillamook Burn as seen in 1933. Today the area is almost fully grown back but travelers along Highway 6 can still look up into the hills and see the white whisker-like remains of groves of trees.

TILLIE FROM TILLAMOOK

Tillamook Tillie got wild one day,
Packed up her things and went away;
She got weary of the birds and bees
And living on Tillamook Cheese:
Tillie, Tillie, Tillie from the Tillamook Bay,
Tillie, Tillie, Tillie!

Silently she stole away
Wooden shoes, a hole in her sock,
Knees that knock-knock, knock-knock,
She's lopsided and she got that way getting up at break of day
Tillie, Tillie, sweeter than the new mown hay!
She's the crash of Broadway today
All dolled up in a sporty shirt
Meadowbrook hat and sawed off skirt.

Tillie says city life's one sweet dream
Three meals a day of pink ice cream;
Her best feller has a saxaphone
And all he can do is to moan:
When they made her village queen
Bugs laid eggs in Tillie's beans.

Everytime they hear her sneeze
Hoot owls shimmy in their B - V- D's.

A "monk" saw Tillie at the zoo
Said: "Long, long time I no see you.

One cold day I had a chill
Tillie led me to a still.

When she dashes down the street
All the cops sing off their beat.

When I met her in the park
I was glad that it was dark.

When she squashes 'round the streets
Parsnips turnup at the beets.

Tillie says she's full of tunes
But we all know she's full of prunes!

By Jack Crowley and Lyn Udall

In December of 1942 the U. S. Naval Air Station developed an airbase for blimps. It was closed after World War II but th[e] two large hangers, each containing seven acres inside, are still permanent landmarks and the largest wood structures in the world.

Along the Oregon Coast fishing has long been a popular sport for fish ranging from the silvery, streamlined salmon to the various species of ungainly looking bottomfish pictured here in this 1937 photo at Netarts.

Patriotism ran high in Tillamook as this post World War I parade demonstrates.

Many buggies were stranded, stuck or tipped but the beach trained horse soon learned to outrun the seventh wave and where to speed up or slow down.

Walking the bridge around Angel Cake Rock at Oceanside was an exciting adventure.

One way of walking to the beach at Oceanside was down the long flight of stairs called "Angels Flight."

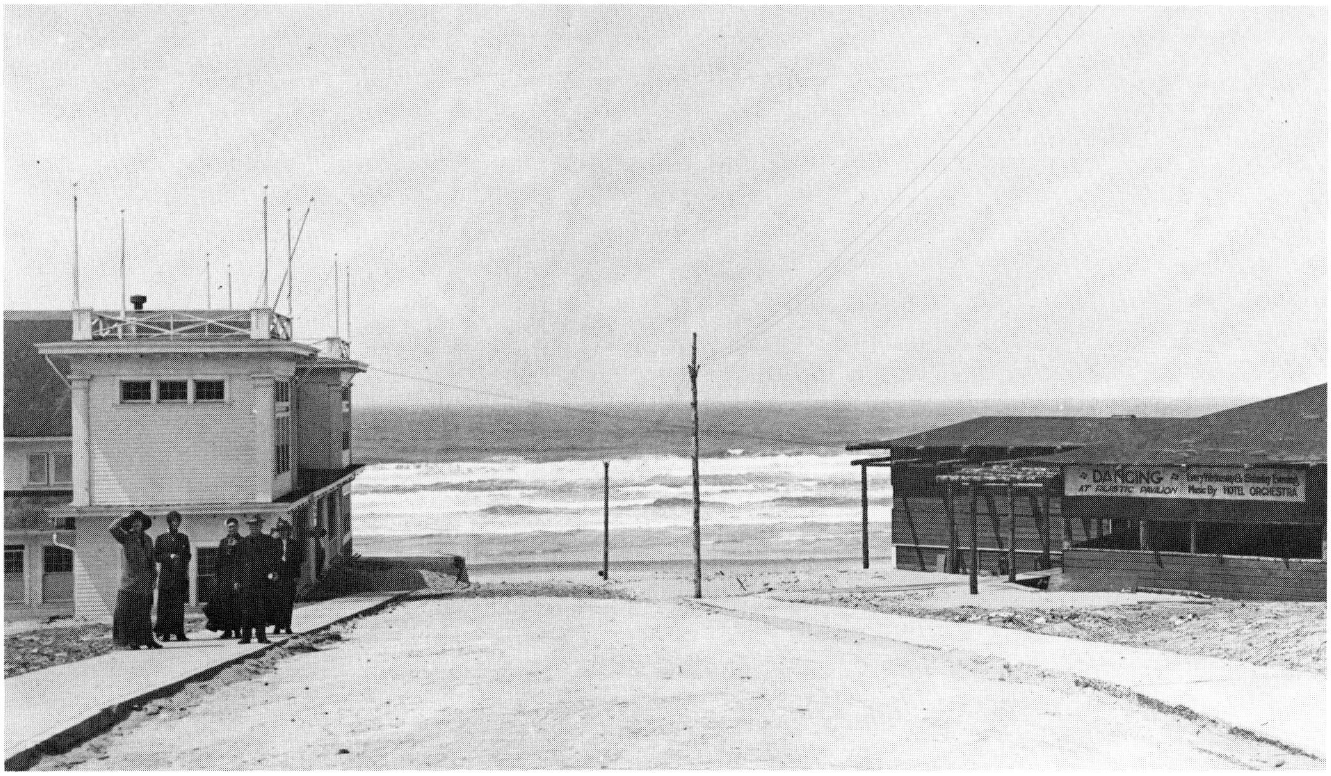
DANCING
AT RUSTIC PAVILION
Music By HOTEL ORCHESTRA

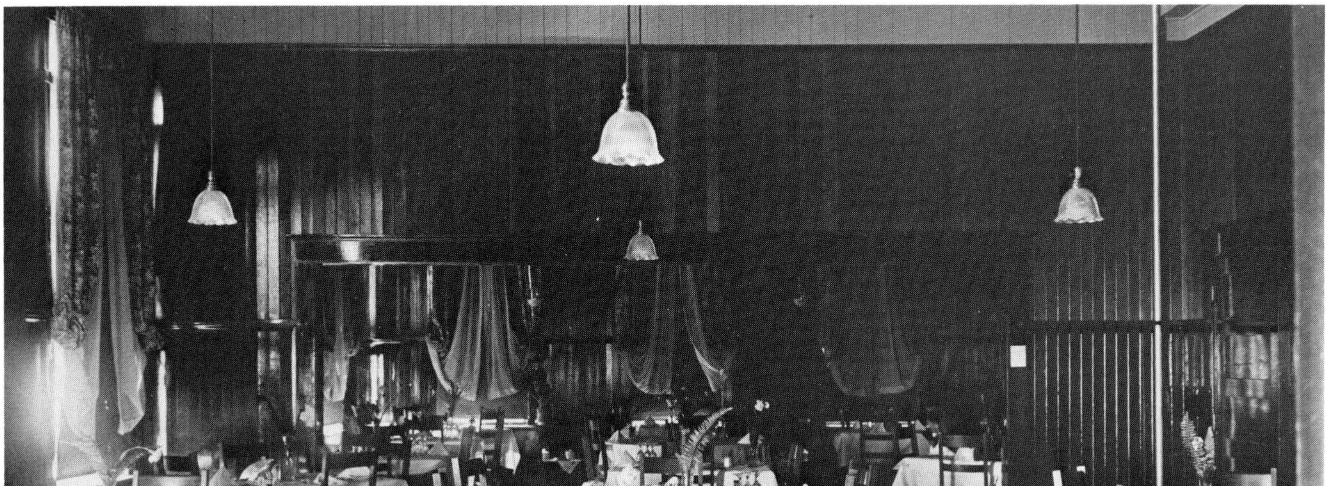

In 1907 Chapin Realty established a summer resort at Bay Ocean near Tillamook. There were three hotels where vacationers stayed from two to four weeks or more. The more elegant Bay Ocean Hotel cost $250,000 to build. In addition, there were tennis courts and a $75,000 natatorium with a 50 by 160 foot tank and seating for one thousand spectators. By 1914 more than 1600 lots were sold, some for as much as $1800. There were several summer homes and some permanent homes that were quite elaborate. The company had already spent $1,200,000 on improvements with more to come. Ferries delivered tourists until 1926 when roads were built to the resort. In 1932 the surf washed away part of the natatorium and the expensive hotel on the hill fell into shambles. By 1939 the natatorium was completely gone and by 1948 the sea was cutting through the peninsula. The last house slid into the ocean in 1960.

Some of the first oyster beds were near Netarts and were owned by Chris Christensen beginning in 1870. Captain Jimmy Winant was the first to establish oyster trade with San Francisco in about 1873. In the early years little regard was given to perpetuating Oregon's resources and many were played out. In the 1870s the last sea otter was shot and oysters suffered overharvest only a few years after they were discovered along the coast. Federal laws now protect the seals and they are making a comeback, oysters are more plentiful and timber harvest is now carefully managed and is an important part of the economy.

Camping along the coast has long been a favorite pastime. This photo, taken in June 1930, is of an auto campground at Seal Rocks. Camps such as this were more primitive and much less convenient than the many state campgrounds along Oregon's coastline today.

Seals tangle fishing nets and eat or scare salmon, thus fishermen's dislike of seals grew and many were shot as this 1895 photo of "Sea Lion" Bob with his gun shows.

These two scenic views of Cape Kiwanda show the rugged coastline that has been used as a backdrop for many "pin-up" pictures throughout the years.

This serene photo of Devil's Lake with row boats and mute swans holds little resemblance to the Indian legend which tells of a giant fish or marine monster living in the lake that would occasionally come to the surface to attack a native — thus the name Devil's Lake.

In 1958 there was a treasure hunt along the Twenty Miracle Miles. One hundred cartons with coupons to be exchanged for silver dollars were buried and thousands of people took part in the hunt.

Buggy rides of one type or another were always fun. This little girl seems to be waiting rather sadly for the next trip.

A division of soldiers was organized on June 15, 1918, and became known as the "Spruce Division." These men and several other squadrons totaling 25,000, were sent to Lincoln County to log spruce for airplane wings. They set up a tent city at South Beach and felled many trees, only to have the war end and the military no longer need the spruce.

Cape Foulweather in Tillamook County is one of the many picturesque lighthouses along the Oregon Coast.

The enormity of the damage done to rivers by logging is amply demonstrated here.

By damming coastal rivers, a large pool could be created which was then filled with logs. Once full, dynamite was used to blow up the dam, creating a flood which carried the logs downstream to tidewater and the lumber mill. The scouring effect of the gigantic logs on the stream bottom gouged steelhead and salmon spawning areas and destroyed much fish life as well. "The environment be damned" might have easily been the motto of the early lumber industry.

Early logging camps were often established in small clearings with a few cabins and an oxen corral. There was little for the men to do in camp but play cards and drink, unless they went into town, an activity usually limited to weekends.

Depoe Bay is the smallest navigable harbor on the Oregon coast. This photo shows Depoe Bay State Park in 1943. Originally this area was included in the Siletz Indian Reservation but later was virtually stolen from the Indians through various land-grab schemes dreamed up by the early pioneers and politicians. The Siletz Tribe included many small groups of Indians from the Chetco River north to the Nestucca River area. Their tribal lands were either seized by the government or purchased for the ridiculous sum of about $1.00 per acre!

This 1867 ad for stage travel to Portland from California points out the risk of ocean travel but many times the overland route proved even more treacherous and less comfortable.

Mail stage rounding Spencer Point in 1915. Sometimes waves would wash over the stage or logs would be thrown into the wheels, thus turning over the stage. The $200.00 per year salary for carriers was well-earned. Life was hard for the horses too and often they lasted only a few years. Stage drivers are Frank Johnson and Sam Hayes.

Originally the township of Newport was jointly owned by Samuel Case and Dr. J. R. Bayley. The township was laid out and named by Samuel Case in 1873. This older photo shows the wagon-tracked main street and harbor that soon became a major fishing community as the later 1923 photo shows. Newport still has canneries, commercial fishing and charter fishing businesses, as well as many other tourist attractions.

Newport's main street in the early 1900s when it was already a thriving coastal town.

Elk and deer are still plentiful along the coast, running in large herds such as this one near Delake.

The popularity of beach activity is evident in this early photo taken at Newport where swimming and car travel on the beach was a common practice. Today cars are not allowed on many of the beaches for safety and conservation reasons.

This large group of Portlanders was enjoying a trip to the beach in 1888. Fishing poles, fish and

72

rifles are clearly evident as well as very formal looking attire!

Rock fishing at Neptune State Park proved to be an enjoyable but sometimes hazardous way to spend the afternoon.

Heceta Head and its lighthouse, built in 1892, is one of the most photographed areas on the coast. It was named for Spanish Captain Bruno Heceta, who was reportedly the first civilized man to sight the opening to the Columbia River on August 17, 1775.

The Oregon sand dunes, near Florence, are fifty-three miles long and two and a half miles wide. The dunes support 135 bird species all year and 430 wildlife species. This National Recreation Area contains 32,185 acres with dunes and lakes for fishing, hunting, boating and dune buggy rides.

The Sea Lion Caves feature a great mainland rookery reachable via a 208-foot elevator that takes visitors down to view the calves and older sea lions resting there. Sea lions were nearly exterminated but are now increasing due to Oregon's protective measures.

Facing page: In some places getting the logs to water for easy transportation was simply a matter of using gravity — and caution.

Trestle accidents were fairly common in the early days of logging due to erosion caused by heavy coastal rainfall, shifting log loads and poor construction. Before the advent of the log truck rails were the primary means for moving the heavy logs to the mills. An observant hiker in the Coast Range today can occasionally spot old grades grown thick with alder and young fir and cedar trees. This trestle went down in November of 1912.

Passengers anxiously waiting at the Marshfield-Drain Stage Line transfer point at Winchester Bay as the steamer comes downstream.

Sailing vessels await their lumber cargo at the docks near Gardiner. Markets for Oregon coastal lumber developed quickly in California after gold was discovered.

Teams of oxen drag a sled of logs down a dusty road in Coos County in the 1880s. By the start of World War II the wood products industry in Oregon employed 120,000 people directly. As early as 1918 responsible lumbermen were proposing reforestation of logged off areas.

Hundreds of large trestles had to be built as log railroads were extended into the steep canyons.

Asa Meade Simpson established the lumber industry in Coos Bay in 1856. Pictured is Simpson's Town Mill. Coos Bay is still the largest lumber shipping port in the world.

One of the finest tellers of oral literature in western Oregon was Annie Miner Peterson, who lived in Coos Bay until her death in the 1930s. She is shown here wearing a cedar bark skirt and a necklace of dentalia shells. These shells came from the west side of Vancouver Island in British Columbia. They played a part in the whole economic and social structure of the western Oregon Indians. Men dreamed of finding large stacks of these shells and women sought dentalia spirit powers. Marriages, disputes and trade were often settled by the exchange of these shells and the wearing of them showed wealth and status.

In addition to sawmills, there were shingle mills, sash and door factories, barrel mills and shipbuilding yards. John McLoughlin, of the Hudson's Bay Company, was the first to initiate shipbuilding in the Northwest in 1826. He was also the first to build a sawmill in 1827.

Crossing the bar at the mouth of the Columbia River has always been hazardous because of the conflicting river and ocean currents, tidal changes, strong winds and shallow, sandy bars. The Columbia bar, in fact, is one of the most dangerous in the world, and has claimed many hundreds of vessels. Here the steamer Admiral Benson is shown in an awkward position after being stranded on Peacock Spit in February, 1930, at the mouth of the Columbia.

In 1913 the Glenesslin sailed into the rocks at the base of Neahkahnie Mountain, with all sails set, on a sunny October afternoon. Some witnesses reported the captain and crew as being quite intoxicated but all made it safely to shore with help from onlookers.

SOME OF THE MANY SHIPWRECKS ALONG THE PACIFIC COAST

The French ship Alice *met its demise during a winter storm in January of 1909 near Ocean Park, Washington. All along the Northwest coast many shipwrecks occurred leaving ghostly looking hulks with their sails ripped by the ferocious winds. Early Spanish and English explorers stayed away from this part of the North Pacific from October until the end of spring.*

This 1851 French map shows the extent of the Oregon Territory before the states of Oregon, Washington and Idaho were carved out. At that time only Astoria was a viable town along the Northwest coastline.

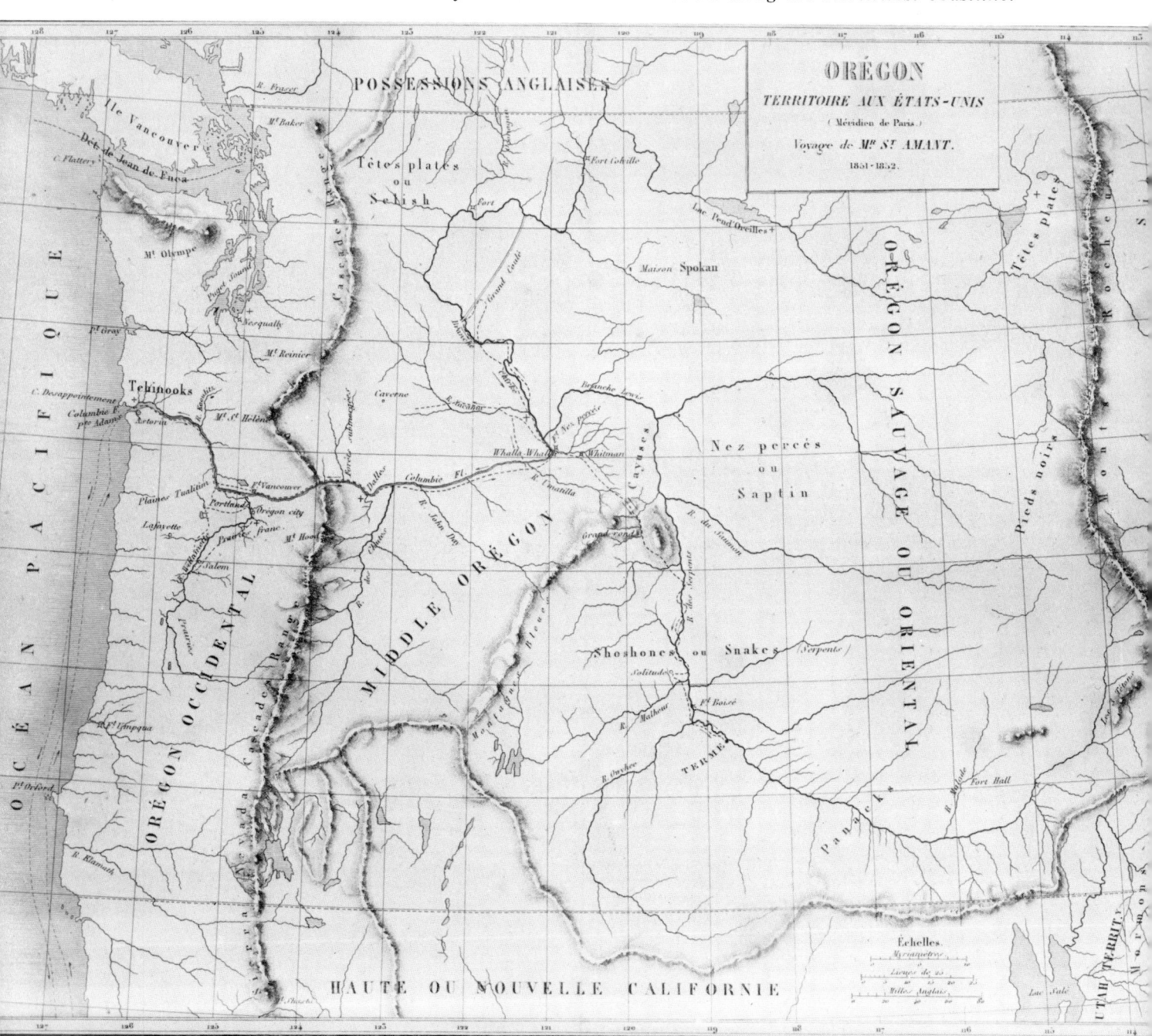

Lighthouse tending was a lonesome job but sometimes an occasional visitor would stop by; only rarely was a lighthouse tended by two men. The quarters were cramped with essentials and the tender had little to do but eat or read when not repairing equipment.

Forty miles south of Florence is Cape Arago with its lighthouse and nearby is Shore Acres featuring an unusual botanical garden. The cape was first sighted by Captain James Cook on March 12, 1778 and named Cape Gregory. It has been called Cape Arago since 1850 in honor of the French physicist and geographer, Dominique Francois Jean Arago (1786-1853).

Powerful waves, mist and just plain beautiful scenery are always there to greet you at the Oregon Coast. The forty miles from Coos Bay to Cape Blanco and Port Orford contain some of the wildest and loneliest stretches along the coastline.

Bandon was named by George Bennett in 1873 after a town of the same name in County Cork, Ireland. In the early 1900s Bandon's waterfront business district was the largest on the Coquille River. The town was almost totally destroyed by fire on September 26, 1936, but was rebuilt and has become the cranberry capital of Oregon. Bandon also features ocean fishing, lumber mills, a cheese factory, and fish hatchery. An Englishman, Billy Buckhorn, is said to have been the first resident of Bandon.

Crossing any of the bars along the Oregon Coast has always been a hazardous adventure. Here a three-masted schooner is attempting to cross the Coquille River bar in 1905.

The rock formation at Bandon is said to show the face of the Indian maiden Ewauna looking skyward away from the "Evil Seatka" and has inspired many stories and poems, one being The Great Stone Face of Bandon *by H. O. Nettleton.*

THE GREAT STONE FACE OF BANDON

In "Wonder Land of Oregon,"
   Of all the states we've got,
A marvel that surpasses all
   Of Nature's sculptor work.
For by the town of Bandon,
   On "The Goddess' Wonder Shore"
Stands a masterpiece of Nature
   in majesty and lure.

'Mid sound that's most enchanting,
   By the mystic sounding caves
Stands "The Great Stone Face of Woman."
   In the breakers' dashing spray

Looking upward into Heaven,
   With features most replete,
It's the wonder of this paradise
   Which pleasure sweethearts seek.

Like a monument erected
   To our Mother Eve, it stands
In the splendor of this Eden
   On the coast of Oregon.
Where the barefoot, lithe sea maiden
   Holds a charm beyond the rose;
And her face reflects the beauty
   Of The Great Stone Face she loves.
                H. O. Nettleton

SOME OF THE STRANGE CREATURES
CAUGHT ALONG THE PACIFIC COAST

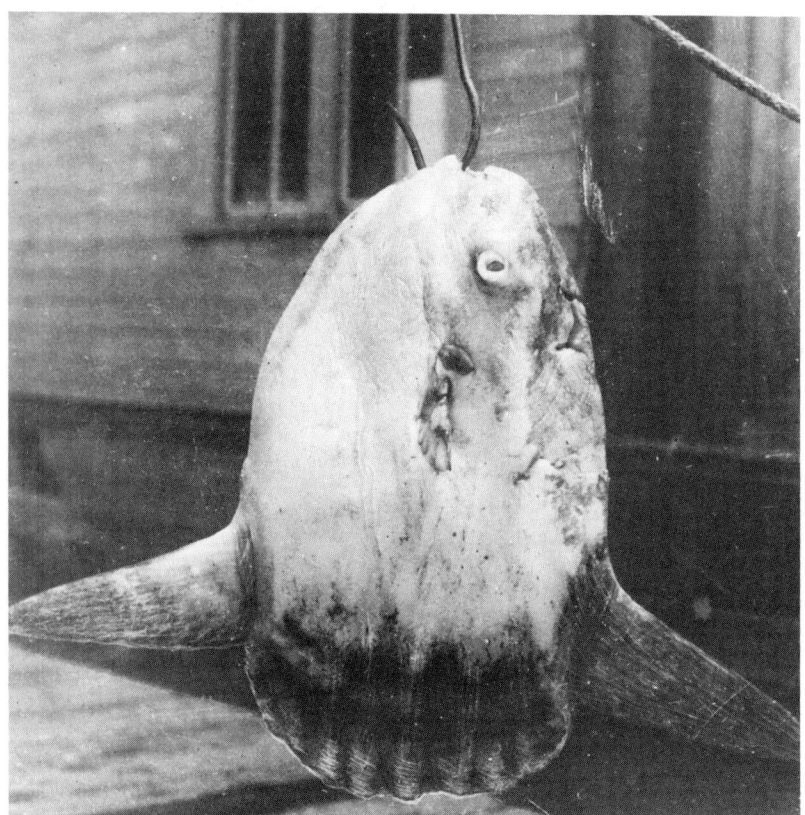

This 500-pound sun fish was caught near the mouth of the Columbia.

This shark was caught off the Oregon Coast near Newport in August of 1913 and weighed in at 5,000 pounds. Warm ocean currents sometimes move close to the Oregon Coast in the summer and bring exotic fish with them.

This rare angler's catch occurred in 1933. The skate weighed 75 pounds and was caught at Barview on July 4th by John W. Wilson (right) and Jack Smith.

In the spring whales migrate along the Oregon Coast northward to British Columbia and Alaska waters. This whale is in the process of being rendered at Grays Harbor Station along the Washington coast.

Bibliography:

Coos Bay Region. Nathan Douthit, River West Books, Coos Bay, Oregon, 1982.

Lincoln County Lore, Lincoln County Historical Society, Newport, Oregon, 1980.

The Indians of Western Oregon, Stephen Dow Beckham, Arago Books, Coos Bay, Oregon, 1977.

The Land That Kept Its Promise. Marjorie H. Hays, Lincoln County Historical Society, Newport, Oregon, 1976.

The Old Oregon Country. Oscar Osburn Winther, Bison Books, Lincoln, Nebraska, 1969.

Tillamook Memories. Tillamook Pioneer Association, Tillamook, Oregon, 1972.

Sentinels of the North Pacific. James A. Gibbs, Jr., Binford & Mort, Portland, Oregon, 1955.

Union Guide to Photograph Collections in the Pacific Northwest, Oregon Historical Society, Portland, Oregon, 1978.

Wildlife of the Pacific Northwest. Margaret McKenny, Arago Books, Coos Bay, Oregon, 1977.

Photo Credits:

All photos are courtesy of the Oregon Historical Society unless otherwise noted. O. H. S. negative numbers are listed by page number.

Front cover, Glenesslin, 16334. 6. Fort George, Columbia Maritime Museum (C. M. M.). 7. Bar at Astoria, C. M. M. 7. Beer truck, Gi9587. 8. Man with large salmon, C. M. M. 9. Square Rigger at Tongue Point, C. M. M. 9. Astoria fire, 57007. 10. Gillnet boat, C. M. M. 10. Fish on boat and barge, 68239. 11. Cannery, Astoria, 28194. 12. Seining, C. M. M. 12. Butterfly fleet, C. C. M. 13. Women at cannery, 54235. 13. Salmon at cannery, Gi7193. 14. Peter Iredale, C. M. M. 15. Wagon pulling car, 35968. 16. Hale Gearhart, 53173. 16. Clam digging, 35633. 17. Cigar raft, 44881. 18,19. Twin Rocks, 72082. 20. Old Main Street, Seaside, 54803. 20. Myricle estate, 72079. 21. Oyster pickers, 36647. 22,23. Boardwalk at Seaside, 56163. 24. Seaside Hotel, 57455. 25. Signpost at Seaside, 72077. 25. Bathers, 64972. 26. Haystack, 73329. 27. Man and woman in surf, 45675. 27. Lifeguards, 52876. 28,29. Sand sculpting, 54797. 30. Tillamook Rock Lighthouse, C. M. M. 31. Storm at Barview, Tillamook Historical Museum (T. H. M.). 32,33. Rockaway, 7106. 34. R. Robinson, T. H. M. 35. Bathing beauties, 38059. 35. Boat Antelope, 26191. 36. Wood road, Tillamook, 58458. 37. Last stage, 25019. 37. Snow storm, T. H. M. 38. Net fishing, 11670. 38. Mail stacked at Tillamook, 25434. 39. Skid road, 54770. 40. Log fleet, 4697. 41. Crib trestle, 26426. 42. Tillamook burn, 9902. 43. Tillamook Burn, 9892. 44. Tillamook Burn, 282756. 45. Hotel Tillamook, T. H. M. 46. Blimps, 37696. 47. Fish caught Netarts, 72080. 47. Parade, T. H. M. 48. Horse and buggy, 17029. 48. Angel Cake Rock, 25806. 49. Angels Flight, 26409. 50 Bay Ocean, 14152. 50. Dining room, 14110. 51. Hotel, 14163. 52. Natatorium, 14165. 53. Natatorium, 14129. 54. Oyster shuckers, Gi7203. 55. Auto campground, 64869. 55. "Sea Lion" Bob, 26402. 56. Cape Kiwanda, 41930. 57. Cape Kiwanda, T. H. M. 58. Devils Lake, 73330. 59. Treasure hunt, 72078. 59. Iron wagon, 73232. 60. Spruce Division, 59331, 55659. 61. Cape Foulweather, 42891. 62. Log jam, 4698. 63. Log flume, 75395. 64. Log camp, 3599. 65. Depoe Bay State Park, 50951. 66. Stage ad, 51751. 67. Mail stage, 54907. 68. Old Newport, 8330. 68. Newport docks, 69776. 69. Mainstreet, Newport, 16807. 70. Elk, 73396. 71. Beach at Newport, 60016. 72,73. Rockfishing, 26854. 74. Neptune State Park, 72081. 75. Heceta Head, 55604, 42198. 76. Florence, 73398. 77. Sea Lion Caves, 73394. 78. Log splash, 3601. 79. Trestle wreck, 36254. 80. Marshfield, steamer, 28241. 80. Ships at Gardiner, 19815. 81. Oxen, 3600. 81. Trestle, 62778. 82. Town mill, 73397. 83. Annie Miner Peterson, T. H. M. 83. Shipyard, 12255. 84. Admiral Benson, C. M. M. 84. Glenesslin, 16334. 85. Alice, C. M. M. 86. Map, 13274. 87. Lighthouse tenders, 12571. 87. Cape Arago lighthouse, 38680. 88,89. Ocean view, 50130. 90. Downtown Bandon, Bandon Historical Museum. 90. Crossing bar, 24442. 91. Stone Face of Bandon, 14096. 92. Sun fish, 59365. 92 Shark. 93. Skate, 59374. 93. Whale, 29586. Back cover, Twin Rocks, 72082.

Columbia River Gorge
Volume One: Discovering Old Oregon Series
Marty Sherman

Columbia River Gorge — the beautiful, rugged gateway that was a terrible obstacle for the pioneers and is now one of our most treasured Northwest possessions. Discover its pictorial history in the just-published book, *Columbia River Gorge*, in the Discovering Old Oregon Series. Shown in striking black and white photos are 110 outstanding scenes photographed from 1867 to 1952.

Starting near Troutdale, Oregon, travel up the Gorge to The Dalles while viewing the old scenic highway, steamboats, rock formations, fish canneries, fishwheels, Rooster Rock, outstanding waterfalls, Indian burial ground islands, tunnels, Indians fishing at once-magnificent Celilo Falls, Cascade Locks and much more. *Columbia River Gorge* is an interesting and informative book enjoyable for all ages.

Bibliography.
8½ by 11 inches, 94 pages.
Softbound: $7.95, ISBN 0-936608-16-1
Hardbound: $18.95, ISBN 0-936608-17-X